Stop Holding on to Your SHI*f*T

Kathryn McKnight

Stop Holding on To Your SHIƒT

Kathryn McKnight

Cover design by Sam4321

Book published by Accountable Actions, LLC.

U.S. Copyright Registration No. 1-7231363561

Printed in the United States of America

ISBN-13: 978-0-578-42707-2

TABLE OF CONTENTS

DEDICATION

I dedicate this book to anyone who wants to grow and move beyond the obstacles blocking them from being the person they're meant to be.

To the younger ones: You don't have to make the same mistakes I made in my high school and college years and even into my twenties and thirties. Every choice you make determines the shape of your future.

This guide will help you FLY (First Love Yourself) and make better choices for a healthier lifestyle. It's never too late to change and become the best possible you. If you remain a student, you will continue to grow. If you stop growing, you will stop living. You deserve to be happy, healthy, and whole. Believe in yourself, take action, and watch the miracles unfold before your eyes.

SPECIAL THANKS

Let me start by thanking God for my second chance at life. It often takes misfortune, tragedy, failure, and a lot of pain to make us step up to the plate and change things for the better.

Thank you to my children for your love, strength, and belief in me. You are my WHY, and because of you I have a burning desire to persevere, prevail, and fight the good fight no matter how many times I'm knocked down. My motto is "Always get back up! Love will conquer all."

Thank you, Mom and Dad, for your support and tough love, for my education, and for instilling faith in me. Most of all, thank you for raising me with integrity, class, morals, and values so that no matter what happens to me, my foundation is rock solid, and I have the will to fight the demons all the way.

Thank you to my siblings Billy, Christine, and Michelle for being strong and loving and trusting the process enough to never let me go. Thank you, Mary, for being my children's second mom when I was in the depths of my addiction.

Thank you, Carol, Laura, Leslie, Janine, Arlene, Mark, Blanca, Kathy, and Carson, for your unconditional love and endless support through the hardest, darkest days of my life. (Never forget who was there for you when you were at your lowest point.) Thank you to all my spiritual family!

Thank you to my life-long friends for always having my back. Thank you to all my mentors, sponsors, and coaches who helped me grow and pursue my dreams. Thank you to all of my children's friends' parents for bringing joy and love to their lives during my hardest struggles.

FOREWORD

From the moment a soul has the grace to know God, she
or he must seek. —Mother Teresa

If you are a seeker of the truth, a seeker of your true self, if you
want to change your life and circumstances to any degree, then
you will enjoy reading Kathy's book and following her steps and
suggestions.

Be prepared to set aside quiet time every day for meditation and
reflection. This may not be part of your daily routine but
committing to it will bring you untold benefits and insights. Be
ready to witness the changes that will occur in your life. But they
will happen in God's time, which may not be on your timetable.

Be prepared to journal. Putting pen to paper gets those ideas out
of your head and onto the page where you can see them and work
on them.

In the intimate reflections in this book, we learn the secrets of
this beautiful woman, the struggles and pain she endured, and
the steps she took and continues to to take become a better,
whole, and inspired woman.

Every time I read this book, I am reminded of my own journey
of self-discovery, one I walk continually as I employ the same
methods to heal through the grace of God, my daily companion.

Arlene Sharpe

INTRODUCTION

I grew up in a traditional American family full of love, faith, and happiness. My parents were devout Catholics of Eastern European and Italian descent. My father was decorated in the Vietnam War and has an enormous entrepreneurial drive, which brought him great financial rewards. My mother, like many women of the Vietnam War era, was a stay-at-home mom, although more recently she has excelled in a managerial leadership career. Our home life was structured, disciplined, and obedient. Dinner, TV, and bedtime were attended by everyone together. We were instilled with the typical values of the time and expected to make our best efforts to adhere to them. Today, my parents remain happily married and our family is close-knit. We share our lives and celebrate together on many traditional occasions.

As an adolescent, I was shy but still popular among my peers. I was an above-average student, an athlete, and a cheerleader, and overall, I was a pretty happy-go-lucky girl. But once the trials of middle school started, I suffered emotional abuse through peer pressure and bullying, and I lost my self-identity. I often asked, "What's wrong with me?" or "Why me?" and wondered if I was somehow different or unworthy. In retrospect, I can see that I lacked the skills and tools to cope with the confusion and heartache I was experiencing. But my first love also happened in my early teens, and it was wonderful and I'm still very grateful for that.

Eventually, I outgrew my first love and became more interested in having fun with my girlfriends. I was a good American girl. I did well in school and didn't get in trouble. But as I grew older and entered high school, I did what everyone else in my town did. I went to parties and drank alcohol. I just wanted to have fun! But the party lifestyle quickly had an impact on my decision-making skills and even my core being. I started dating the wrong type of men, and I didn't know how to choose better. With time, my poor choices destroyed my self-esteem.

The men I chose were dishonest, unfaithful, unavailable, and even substance abusers. They also lacked the skills to build intimate relationships. Rather than walking away from these red flags, though, I became a victim, full of anger, resentment, insecurity, and pain. It became a pattern, and I adopted the role of a serial long-term partner. I would remain in abusive, unfaithful, and unhealthy relationships while I tried to fix and control men and teach them how to treat me. I was always angry and disappointed.

If I only knew then what I know now! But I was a mess. Burdened with pain and confusion, I would commit to men who didn't know how to treat women. The longer I tolerated unhealthy relationships, the sicker I became. And to add to the nausea, I married one!

I often turned to alcohol and drugs to ease my pain. Eventually, my substance abuse took control of my life. Despite the way I courted disaster, I was blessed with three beautiful, amazing children who mean the world to me. But I disliked myself as a mother, and I hated the man I had married. I felt betrayed and angry with myself for choosing a man who was incapable of doing the right thing by me and our children.

I know now that men felt betrayed, hurt, and mistreated by me too. I was angry, and I would assault them with painful words and remind them of their ugly truths. At some point I realized that if I had any self-respect or self-love, I wouldn't have needed to waste such time fighting losing battles.

I knew that I had a lot of work to do, and I spent countless hours sitting on my porch analyzing my life and trying to escape my dilemmas. I was sick and tired of feeling sick and tired. I'd had enough of feeling like a loser, always sad, lost, and angry, and I was ready to change. And miraculously, I awoke one day with a new attitude. God whispered in my ear, "You need to do something about this vicious cycle."

I had no idea that I was completely disconnected from God. I had let go of God, opting for the self-defeating attitude of "my will, my way." But I soon discovered that God had never let go of me. God gave me the direction I needed and wanted. Although I took the long way due to my stubborn, egotistical, and victimized ways, I never gave up, no matter how many times I regressed through self-sabotage or relapse. And my journey has unfolded just as it was supposed to.

I've always had a vision of who I wanted to be—as a woman, a mother, a soulmate, a daughter, a sister, a friend, even an employee. The changes started in my late 30s, with what I think of as baby steps. But actions speak louder than words, and my vision quickly started to become a reality.

As I said, I'm Catholic. I've always attended mass and confession. My prayers have always been heart-felt. I feel I have a rock-solid ability to follow the golden rule and do the right thing. God led me to a twelve-step program, though I still went through years of denial before I was ready to see the truth about myself. My fears, my reasons for behaving the way I did, and my growing through what I faced were quite the process. But I have an amazing mentor, a life coach who guides me with grace, wisdom, and God's will.

By acting, working through, and trusting the process, I learned to heal my past and right my wrongs. I repaired many relationships just by changing myself. I no longer carry the baggage of my past or any unnecessary pain. I am free and more secure, happy, and healthy than I've ever been. My kids have a healthy mother, and I'm friends with my exes. I even co-parent well with my children's father today. I no longer view situations from a victim's mindset. I am 100% accountable for my actions and my life.

God has inspired me to share my journey. I am hoping that through it, others will find peace, love, and joy. The steps I followed led to results in every part of my life. I have outlined these steps, which can turn anyone's life around. They're miraculous! I went from being broken, lost, angry, and blaming others, to a wholeness like a vision of heaven. I am happy, content, and secure, and I'm fully accountable for everything I create along my journey. If these steps worked for me, they will work for anyone. This process will change your life entirely and pull you from the depths of darkness into the light of joy.

It's your turn now. You are worth it!

STEP 1

IDENTIFY THE PROBLEM

This is the first step in your quest to becoming a better person. It is the most important part of the journey. Before you start thinking about a better you, you must ruminate on what the problem is with your personality. Who are you? What do you do that keeps disrupting your life? What weaknesses and character flaws do you ignore or overlook? Are you in self-denial because you're afraid of the truth? It's time to identify the culprits who are standing in the way of your growth, success, and joy. Identifying the problem will give you the opportunity to make corrections and set yourself on the right track before you take any other steps.

Who are you?

This stage of the journey starts with understanding who you are at your core. This means becoming in tune with your deeper self so that you recognize what disturbs you and what makes you happy or sad. How do you deal with your emotions? How do you react when life goes astray? What are your negative qualities? What do you excel in? What do you need to work on in your personal growth and development? When we truly understand ourselves, we can make a conscious effort to improve and communicate better with others.

Maybe your problems are obvious. But here are a few reasons you might want to know your nature.

- **Happiness.** You will be happier when you can be true to yourself. Being in touch with your wishes and desires will help you have your needs met.

- **Less inner conflict.** When you're confident in your words and in who you are, your thoughts and actions will be congruent, and you will feel secure and at peace with your choices.

- **Better decisions.** When you know yourself, you'll make better choices about everything from which sweater you'll buy to which partner you'll spend your life with. It's magical!

- **Self-control.** After you work through these steps, you'll understand your triggers and be able to control your emotions instead of allowing them to control you. You will find positive solutions to life's challenges rather than answering them with negative behaviors. You will allow your feelings to flow. You will honor them with love and care rather than regret. Bad habits and self-sabotage will be diminished. You'll have the insight to know which values and goals activate your will power.

- **Resistance to social pressure.** When you're grounded in your values and preferences, you are less likely to say yes when you want to say no.

- **Tolerance and understanding.** Your awareness of your own shortcomings and struggles can help you empathize and be more patient with others.

- **Vitality and pleasure.** Staying joyful leads to a healthy, strong life full of abundance. The more enthusiastic you are about your life, the more exciting your life will become.

Denial (= Don't Even No I Am Lying)

This is a major problem that hinders people from improving and achieving their dreams. We've all been unhappy with choices we've made. We've all felt in our hearts that we could have done better. Making mistakes is a part of being human. I have made plenty in my lifetime. But what happens when our mistakes become patterns? Are the same mistakes holding you back again and again?

With self-denial, you are subconsciously blocking yourself from the joy you deserve. Sometimes we need to go within to explore why we're denying ourselves the goodness that would come from breaking our old patterns. When we do so, what we focus on expands.

Keep your mind on the positive, and picture your life the way you want it to look. Create a wonderful vision of your dream life. Then take action to make it real. Keeping a positive attitude, believing in yourself, and speaking healthy affirmations will help you create the life you envision. You are what you think, so only think good thoughts. The law of attraction starts with our thoughts and beliefs.

Denial has a dark side with severe consequences. It's a coping mechanism that gives you time to adjust to distressing situations but staying in denial can interfere with your ability to tackle challenges.

If you're in denial, you're trying to protect yourself by refusing to accept the truth about something. Sometimes, short-term denial is a good thing. And it can be a precursor to making positive changes. Refusing to acknowledge that anything is wrong is one way of coping with emotional conflict, stress, painful thoughts, threatening information, and anxiety. You can be in denial about anything that makes you feel vulnerable or threatens your sense of control, such as illness, addiction, eating disorders, violence, financial problems, or relationship conflicts. You can be in denial about something happening to you or to someone else. Find out when denial is unhealthy and affecting your life negatively through these steps.

Moving Past Self-Denial

When you are faced with an overwhelming turn of events, it's okay to say, "I just can't think about all this right now." You might need time to work through what happened and adapt to the new circumstances. But it's important to remember that denial can only be a temporary measure: it won't change the reality of the situation.

It isn't always easy to tell whether denial is holding you back. The strength of denial can change over time, especially when challenges linger. Some bouts of denial are linked to being less defensive. When denial grows stronger and harder, it can delay breakthroughs.

If you feel stuck, or someone you trust suggests that you're in denial, try these strategies:

- Examine your feelings in depth and honestly.

- Think about the possible consequences of not taking the right action.

- Let yourself express your fears and emotions.

- Identify irrational beliefs (intrusive thoughts) you might have about your situation.

- Journal about your experiences.

- Communicate openly to a trusted friend or loved one.

- Participate in a support group.

If you can't make progress with a stressful situation on your own, you can end up stuck in the denial phase and needing to find a pathway out.

You deserve all the goodness life has to offer. But denial is so powerful that it can rob you of all the good things you deserve. The results you will achieve by taking action to step out of denial are happiness, joy, and freedom.

Recognizing Your Strengths and Weaknesses

Addressing your strengths and weaknesses is imperative. But many people struggle to even know what their own strengths and weaknesses are.

Logically speaking, strength is the absence of weakness, and vice versa. And we try to build up our strengths and reduce our weaknesses. But we often go in circles, never quite succeeding at either.

Really, strength isn't the absence of weakness. Weakness is just the mirror image of strength, and vice versa. They are the very same thing, and you can't have either without the other.

Perhaps you live by principles but are still judgmental. Or you're easily hurt but also compassionate. You're focused but often one-dimensional. You're creative but a hot mess. Maybe you're pragmatic but also a total bore. You're humble, but you let others walk all over you. Maybe you're passionate but manic, greedy but too generous, or brave but very foolish.

You may recognize aspects of yourself in these characteristics. Strengths and weaknesses are just two aspects of one and the same thing. When we try to divide them, we fail at both. We live by principles, so we try to be less judgmental. We're compassionate but too sensitive, so we try to be thicker-skinned and then we lose our gentleness. Understand that the stronger you are, the less weak you become. We can't divide the two: they're one.

Knowing your strengths and weaknesses gives you a better understanding of yourself and how you function. We only grow when we know what our weaknesses are. We must be vulnerable, open-minded, and ready to change the way we perceive situations and even personal beliefs of ours that often knock us down. We have to approach these challenges wearing a new set of God goggles. Our attitudes will make us or break us.

Understanding your strengths keeps you on top of your game in many ways. For instance, if you're looking at career options, you can narrow down the scope of your list to specific jobs based on the things you know and are passionate about. Knowing what you excel at lets you aim higher and achieve more. Knowing your weaknesses gives you a clearer understanding of what's holding you back. You can then work around your weaknesses and find ways to keep them from pulling you down.

Self-Discovery

The best way to understand who you are is to undertake the process of self-discovery. This is a lifelong journey of exploration through your inner self as you try to discover who you are, your potential, your purpose in life, and the core principles that guide you down the different paths you take along the way. The journey begins with self-awareness then moves into personal interests and hopes and dreams for the future. It eventually leads to self-knowledge, which enables you to guide yourself toward situations and experiences in which you will thrive.

> What lies behind us and what lies before us are tiny matters compared to what lies within us. —Oliver Wendell Holmes

Self-discovery is a fundamental component of personal growth. We must each take the time to discover who we are as a person. This is accomplished through self-reflection. Self-reflection allows us to examine our actions, preferences, feelings, values, beliefs, and tendencies. Because we all think, feel, act, learn, and perceive the world differently, taking the time to reflect helps us gain a better insight into ourselves. Self-discovery is a way to explore our individual personalities, natural preferences, values, beliefs, preferred styles, and tendencies. The ultimate destination of this journey is finding out who we are and what makes us unique.

Self-discovery is a process of being guided, through self-questioning and examination of one's thoughts, words, and actions, toward conclusions about who one truly is. Through this process, you can gain a deeper understanding of yourself and your character traits, values, and true purpose in life. It allows you to live to your fullest potential.

The first step in the self-discovery process is self-reflection. You must make the time to stop and think about who you are. Quiet meditation and reflection will allow you to refocus your mind, concentrate on your inner self, and examine the way you see yourself. This lets you to explore your personality, natural preferences, values, beliefs, preferred styles and tendencies in order to become more self-aware. You can also reflect on your interests and dreams and what you would like to do for a living.

STEP 2

BELIEVE IN GOD

It's a sign of the times that we want to become better people. We can set goals for ourselves, as long as we're pursuing them for the right reasons and in the right ways. Sometimes the goals we set are unrealistic or even just wishful thinking. We face a deeper problem when our goals are realistic and we know how to reach them but we still fail—something you may have experienced. One of the biggest causes of this kind of failure is the belief that we can do it all alone. Most of us think we can handle everything by ourselves without help from God.

We think this because we lack the moral and spiritual strength within us to do what's right. Even the Apostle Paul had to say, "I do not do the good I want to do, but the evil I do not want to do—this I keep on doing" (Romans 7:19).

This is why we need God's help: Only he can give us the strength we need to live the way we should. You must believe that there is something greater than you. You must rely on a higher power when you try to become a better person. The higher power that I use, and the one I recommend to you, is God.

What Is Trust?

The Merriam-Webster dictionary defines trust as "the belief that someone or something is reliable, good, honest or effective." We all know that God is the full embodiment of this definition and much more. So why is it so hard for us to believe him?

19

I believe it's because our society has programmed us to not trust anyone or anything. We all know the phrase, "too good to be true." When we use it, we mean that the better someone is or the better something sounds, the more likely we are to find fault in it due to our disbelief. This often becomes second-nature and we don't even realize that we're doing it. It becomes embedded in our subconscious. But it isn't the case with God: God is never too good to be true. In fact, God wants to surprise us in a BIG way.

Believing in God isn't always second nature, but it's imperative for having a solid, healthy, trusting foundation to live on. When times are tough and things aren't going your way, you have to fully trust God in blind faith.

In reality, though, you doubt that God will come through for you. You lack faith in his promises, you worry endlessly about your future, and you project outcomes that may never happen, until you're left feeling depleted and drained. The problem is that this is exactly the opposite of how God wants you to react to the difficulties in your life. God wants you to trust him when you have doubts and are unsure what to do. He wants you to believe in his promises when you think that things are going to get worse.

This seems difficult: how can you trust God when you feel like trusting God is impossible? You might be surprised to learn that trust is like a muscle. The more that you exercise your faith, the more it strengthens and grows. Here are two exercises to strengthen your trust muscle.

1. Surrender yourself and all your troubles to God. When you realize that there's a supernatural strength available to you, your perspective on life will change. You can move from worry to worship by remembering that God is in control of every circumstance in your life. Let God be the master of your actions, thoughts, and behaviors toward everything in your life. Once you stop trying to do things with your own strength, God will take over and lift you to higher levels.

2. Replace negative thoughts with positive ones. Your thoughts are extremely powerful and can affect your mood, your attitude, and your actions. When you find negative thoughts bringing you down, start thinking about positive scriptures that will lift you up. You can do this by memorizing some of your favorite passages. For example:

> "Trust in the Lord with all your heart and lean not on your own understanding; in all your ways submit to him, and he will make your paths straight." — Proverbs 3:5

Repeat verses that lift your spirits like the one above. Continue until your negative thoughts are replaced with God's peace, transcending your limited beliefs with security and self-worth. Believe that God will come through for you at the moment you need him too, and God will never fail you, forsake you, or leave you. Persevere with prayer during this time because your faith will be tested. During your trial, ask God to give you patience and to help you trust that he knows what's best for you. Remember, God always shows up right on time.

Asking God to help you achieve your desires begins with

committing yourself to his commandments. Trusting him every day to guide you toward the person he wants you to be is a true representation of faith. Trust God with your life, and expect good things to happen to you. Expect greatness. Expect God's favor in all things.

This doesn't mean that life will be rainbows and butterflies all the time, but it does mean that God will deliver you out of every situation you're in. If God brings you to it, God will bring you through it. Know that God can work miracles on your behalf, and he will move mountains for you. All you have to do is trust him, and you can rest assured that your journey to being a better person will have a dependable driver. God will make your trip smoother than you yourself ever could.

STEP 3

BE WILLING TO PUT EVERYTHING IN GOD'S HANDS

This step is similar to the second one. Once you believe that God will assist you in your quest to be a better person, you must be willing to put everything in his care. This willingness starts with the decision to open yourself to God by surrendering your past, present, and future to him.

> "The submission of one's will is really the only uniquely personal thing we have to place on God's altar. It is a hard doctrine, but it is true. The many other things we give to God however nice that may be of us are things he has already given us. He has loaned them to us. But when we begin to submit ourselves by allowing our will to be swallowed up in God's will then we are really giving something to him." ("Insights from My Life," *Ensign*, Aug. 2000, 9)

Without a doubt, the greatest discovery of your life will be when you finally have the total confidence to walk hand-in-hand with God, to let God help you through every obstacle and problem life throws in your way. You will be able to surrender your life to him without hesitation, doubt, or unrealistic expectations. When you take step 3, you demonstrate your willingness to surrender your thoughts and actions to God's care. This willingness to put everything in God's hands and let him God to take charge of your life will make you better than ever. It is a decision to allow God to direct your life in the knowledge that he will

23

always do what is best for you. You choose to put your life in God's hands when you follow his lead, and your willingness is the foundation on which your success is built. When you take this step, you may be terrified of the unknown. What would happen if you humbled yourself and surrendered your will and your life completely to the care of God?

Believing that God can make you better showms courage and faith. I believe "courage" is the right word in this situation. After all, it's not easy to hand your stress and worries over to God. That would mean that you aren't in control, right?

Stop and ask yourself this question: Is it better for God or me to be in control of my own life? Martin Luther King once said, "I have held many things in my hands and I have lost them all; but whatever I have placed in God's hands, that I still possess." What he meant is that if you want to make God laugh, tell him about your plans.

When you try to control things, you aren't letting God take the wheel. What you give to God will be handled with care. If you don't release your issues, fears, and will into God's care, you'll lose everything you're trying to control. But if you hand them over to God, he'll help you keep what you need. God will make your plans prosper and develop them to serve your life's purpose. When you put your plan in God's hands, he will put peace in your heart. You will no longer need to carry the burdens of your uncertainties. God will carry them all, and you will be successful no matter what situation you face.

God is aware of your situation and using it for his ultimate glory. When you're feeling overwhelmed, hopeless, afraid as if you're drowning in worry believing that you will never get better, let go let god in, step back, hand everything over to God and watch God bring you to a place of relief, belief and peace. It sounds so simple but you have to keep the faith, take this action step in order for it to work. I promise you he knows what he's doing. Our ability to withstand temptation is now grounded in our continual submission to the will of the Lord. We express our need for the power available to us through the Saviors Atonement and we begin to feel that power within fortifying us for the next task ahead. Continued submission to God's will reduces fear, worry, anxiety, stress and all negative emotions bringing more meaning to your lives. You no longer fear the future and you're able to accept responsibility for your actions. You're completely confident that self-will is no challenge against God's will for your life. Self-will always have the potential to bring you sorrow and frustration vs God's will which will be bringing you happiness and peace.

Each new day we renew our submission to the Lord and His will. This is what most of us mean when we say, "one day at a time." We have decided to let go of our self-will, self-seeking ways that were at the root of our self-obsession. You may enjoy another 24 hours of the serenity and strength that comes from trusting God and his goodness, power, and love.

Benediction and Final Greetings

Now may the God of peace, who through the blood of the eternal covenant brought back from the dead our Lord Jesus, that great Shepherd of the sheep, equip you with everything good for doing his will, and may he work in us what is pleasing to him, through Jesus Christ, to whom be glory for ever and ever. Amen.

—Hebrews 13:20-21

STEP 4

MAKE YOURSELF ACCOUNTABLE

Holding yourself accountable is nothing more than following through on your commitments and responsibilities. It's doing what you know you should do when you should do it. But being accountable is more than just being responsible for something. It's also being answerable for your actions. To hold yourself accountable, you must find the motivation to do difficult things. When you make a mistake, you must own it. This will restore people's confidence and trust in you.

As soon as you take ownership of your actions and understanding why being fully accountable matters, you will become the kind of person who attracts others. When we make excuses, when we blame other people or external factors for the outcomes of our actions, not only do fail to take responsibility, we demonstrate a character trait that is common among people who fail at everything.

In shouldering responsibility, you give yourself the power to shape the outcome. You take an active and not a passive role in the outcome.

Realization

It's only when you accept that everything you are or will be is within your power that it becomes your choice. Being accountable lets you determine whether you will eliminate negativity or create it in your life. Making excuses can prevent you from succeeding. You may find yourself in an unhappy position because you blame everyone else instead of looking within. But we all have free will, and that means we're responsible for all our successes and failures and for our happiness or unhappiness.

At first, this can seem like a huge responsibility to take onto our shoulders. But when you fully accept that you are responsible for every action you take and every decision you make, there is virtually nothing that you can't do, have, or achieve.

Accepting responsibility has two basic components. The first is accepting personal responsibility. That means taking ownership of your behavior and its consequences. Until you take responsibility for your actions and failures, it will be hard for you to develop self-respect or even gain the respect of others. It's a simple truth that all human beings make mistakes and poor choices. We all sometimes fail to act when we know we should. There are times when we all look the other way even though we know the right thing to do is help. So remember, first of all, that you're not the first person who has fallen short in your personal behavior from time to time.

The second component is accepting indirect responsibility. This involves moving beyond yourself and acting to help other people or situations around you that call for assistance. Indirect responsibility may not rise to the level of personal responsibility, but it does reveal something about your character and the type of person you are. Many people will walk right by the person who is down in the street or down on his luck. But there are others, thank goodness, who'll quickly stop and try to help. It's not hard to decide which of these is the responsible choice.

The real difference between being responsible and being irresponsible is how well we manage our lives when the opportunity to make a good or bad choice presents itself. Accepting responsibility, both personally and indirectly, is one of the most important and defining factors in a person's true character. When that moment of responsibility comes, what you do or don't do is a sign of the type of person you truly are. You grow when you get out of your comfort zone.

Self-Inventory

A major way of making yourself accountable is to take stock of your characteristics and attributes. A personal inventory of your unique traits can help you determine your future. It can help you figure out how your skills, experiences, strengths, weaknesses, goals, and interests all fit together. By getting a better sense of your moral inventory, you can figure out who you are and what you have to offer.

Many people wish for self-development but freeze up when the time comes to act. Not every wish needs to be explored but taking the time to figure out what your dreams are and how you fit into them can help you uncover your potential, and a self-inventory can help you explore who you are in depth.

Mother Teresa's Anyway Poem

People are often unreasonable, illogical and self centered;

Forgive them anyway.

If you are kind, people may accuse you of selfish, ulterior motives;

Be kind anyway.

If you are successful, you will win some false friends and some true enemies;

Succeed anyway.

If you are honest and frank, people may cheat you;

Be honest and frank anyway.

What you spend years building, someone could destroy overnight;

Build anyway.

If you find serenity and happiness, they may be jealous;

Be happy anyway.

The good you do today, people will often forget tomorrow;

Do good anyway.

Give the world the best you have, and it may never be enough;

Give the world the best you've got anyway.

You see, in the final analysis, it is between you and your God;

It was never between you and them anyway.

STEP 5

ELIMINATING OBSTACLES THAT BLOCK YOUR SHIfT

Humans are essentially creatures of habit. What you choose to eat and how much, what time you go to bed and what time you wake up, your conduct, temperament, and so many other actions stem from habits, good or bad.

Good habits help you carry out everyday functions and improve your relationships with others. These include keeping proper hygiene, greeting elders kindly, respecting people in authority, and showing common courtesy to others. You build a good habit by doing the right thing repeatedly until it is a part of you.

Over time, wrong actions can also become a part of you. Bad habits can injure you and others. They include overeating, skimping on sleep, leaving your home messy, procrastinating, arriving late to appointments, losing your temper, being crude, borrowing money constantly, drinking too much, being negative, and gossiping. Bad habits can be difficult to break, but you can learn to overcome them. Remember, habits aren't what you are; they're what you allow yourself to become.

Having a bad character is like writing with a pen. It's easy to write on a blank sheet, but it's hard to erase what's been written. Likewise, it's easier to form a new positive habit than to break an old negative one. Once an act is a part of your routine, it's difficult for the brain to change it. And the more you act, the more you do it without thinking, the harder it gets; it's a vicious cycle.

How to Overcome

By allowing God's Spirit to live in you, you can remove the old you and embrace the new you.

Character defects have the effect of dimming our lights and preventing us from shining brightly as a beacon to help others find their way. By asking God to remove our negative behavior traits, we cleanse our souls and allow our healthiest selves to shine forth. The bad traits we carry corrupt us and can harm those around us, so we must take radical action against to remove this and not allow it to permeate our spiritual lives:

> Get rid of the old yeast, so that you may be a new unleavened batch—as you really are. For Christ, our Passover lamb, has been sacrificed. —I Corinthians 5:7.

A good way to begin is through introspection. Find time to take an inventory of your behaviors and where you stand. For instance, if you struggle with weight, ask yourself this: "Am I truly dissatisfied with my weight and my health, or just feeling guilty after over-indulging in a meal? How does my current health affect my family and friends in the short term? and in the long term? What role am I playing in making the problem better or worse?" This is just an example of the challenges you might face. The point is that carefully examining the root causes of unwanted behavior will help us discover our weaknesses.

You can overcome bad habits if you set your mind to it.

A good practice for remaining right-minded and healthy is to stay vigilant about your actions. This can mean observing the examples of others, including friends and family members, who are good at what you are striving for. The key is to focus on learning and changing and to apply the lessons you learn to improve your own life consistently.

Here are some more practical ways to form good habits:

1. Admit that you have a bad habit. This begins in the introspection stage, but it's important to identify your habits and recognize those that you need to change. The brain may be resistant to change, but change is possible if you resist pride and humbly acknowledge your faults.

2. Understand the reasons for the habit. To stop a behavior, you must identify the reasons behind it. Human nature always plays a large part, but there may be other factors. These could include your upbringing, fears, or other bad experiences. Finding these will help you sincerely evaluate the cause of the problem and better see the need to overcome it.

3. Write down everything, including reasons to change. One approach is to draw two vertical lines on a notebook page so that you have three columns. On the left, list all your bad habits. In the middle, list the reasons for each one. On the right, list the reasons you want to kick each habit. This exercise can be very rewarding: putting pen to paper will help you see your weaknesses and strengths and make it easier to resolve to remove the bad habits.

4. Learn to despise the bad habit. You can stop a bad habit more easily if you're tired of the results it brings. If you hate it enough, you'll be able to muster the strength to fight it and resist returning to your old ways. A reluctance to change negative thoughts often makes people return to bad habits. Instead, you must take control even over your thoughts.

5. Believe and be determined to overcome the habit. The urge to continue negative behavior can be overpowering, but the truth is that you can overcome it. Why? Because God says so!

Step 6

LET IT GO

Sincerely apologizing to the people you have harmed, whether today or yesterday, brings relief. If you want to become a better version of yourself, you must not let past mistakes pull you back or destroy the new you that you're creating. You may have stepped on some toes while struggling with the old you, so it's time to revisit them and make amends.

Your relationships with your loved ones are a major part of your life. If you find out that you've hurt one of these people, knowingly or unknowingly, you need to mend the relationship with with a complete, healing apology that addresses their pain and possible need for retaliation. You do this by saying sorry, right? Well, what if I tell you that "sorry" is a big word that can mean a lot — or nothing at all?

Sometimes saying you're sorry just isn't good enough, especially if you've said it a hundred times before.

We've all heard the advice "Just put it behind you and move on." But when you hurt someone to their core, a simple "I'm sorry" is just the start of repairing the relationship. It might make you feel better, but for the other person it can just leave a feeling of uncertainty. They still must carry their disappointment and scars while you get to move on feeling free.

Here are some reasons you should make restitution. It's a matter of obedience.

- **The Bible treats restitution as part of your daily**

obedience to God. The reason we don't like this isn't that it's unbiblical. It's because it's opposed by our pride. We hate to be humbled, embarrassed, humiliated, or wrong especially when we're focusing on the other' person's part in an incident. It makes us focus on ourselves, which goes against our nature. We would rather save face than make amends. But the problem remains unresolved as long as we are slow in our obedience. The single best reason to make restitution is because it is God's will for us. It's a matter of obedience.

- **Restitution reinforces personal happiness.** When we leave a restitution unmade, we add a load of guilt to our daily burdens. Once we've made things right, that load of sadness, shame, and guilt is lifted from us. When we push our unrighted wrongs out of sight, they resurface and cause us to relive our awful feelings of guilt and shame. Once we've made restitution, we experience a new happiness and freedom in our lives. Then we wonder why we took so long to do it in the first place. You'll be a happier and holier person after you've made amends.

- **Restitution removes another person's stumbling block.** Has it occurred to you that someone might hold a grudge against you for something you said or did a long time ago? Have you ever thought that someone might still be sour, bitter, and full of resentment over that little thing you did? What would happen if you approached them and humbly asked for forgiveness? And what if they gave it—could they still hold a grudge? You aren't an accessory to their sin of unforgiveness, but your tardiness in making restitution may be a stumbling block in their path toward God's will.

- **Restitution protects the offended against future wrongs.** Nothing can guarantee that you won't slip and fall again, but restitution comes close. The next time you're tempted to take something that doesn't belong to you, you'll remember the past pain and humiliation of returning to make restitution. The next time you're about to let loose with a biting, sarcastic, remark, you'll think of the embarrassment in store later when you have to ask the person to forgive you. These thoughts are a preventative medicine. A little pain now—doing without or biting your tongue—is preferable to the greater pain of making restitution.

How to Make Genuine Restitution

1. Acknowledge. Seeing how your actions affect others is the key to making a sincere apology. The acknowledgment part of the apology needs to start with "I." For example, "I'm sorry for being late tonight."

2. Empathize and feel remorse. Remorse is truly feeling bad about what you've done. Empathy is being able to put yourself in the other person's shoes and know how they feel. The remorse and empathy parts of an apology sound like this: "Lisa, I'm sorry I said that to you. I don't like myself for being so reactive, and I know from when my own family members are harsh or judgmental just how much it can hurt."

37

3. Make Amends. Provide an act or service to make up for the transgression. Consider a husband who's short and abrupt with his wife when she's excited to tell him about her first day at a new job. He can provide restitution by offering to listen better after making her a cup of tea and doing some extra housework while she relaxes.

It's important to mend a damaged relationship in a meaningful way. Back up your apology with actions. Expressions of regret mean a lot more when you provide pathways to change and, even better, follow them. Apologizing involves more than saying "I'm sorry." It's important to open communication channels and listen to how you hurt the other person. Once you've restored your connection, you can start fixing the situation by taking responsibility for the harm you caused and doing whatever's necessary to correct it. Only then can you begin to restore the victim's feelings of self-worth.

> If you don't like something, change it. If you can't
> change it, change your attitude. —Maya Angelou

> Nothing is impossible, the word itself says 'I'm possible.'
> —Audrey Hepburn

STEP 7

COME BACK STRONGER

If there's one thing I know, it's that life will never cease to surprise and amaze us. One minute your world is perfectly aligned and carrying on smoothly. Your relationship is solid. Your job is fulfilling. Your health is strong. Then out of nowhere, a serious wrench is thrown into the works. Your once faultlessly balanced life starts falling apart.

I've had my share of "Oh no, what's next?" moments. None of them were expected, but they happened and I had to deal with them. Once, a person I trusted betray me with lies and deceit. I definitely didn't sign up for that. Another time, I was completely blindsided by a break-up with someone I thought could be the one. However, all these terrible events had something in common: a fresh start.

It's easy to look at an unfortunate event as a loss or a failure, yet they can be so much more. They can be learning experiences. It can be hard to view things that way during troubled times, but trust me, the truth is hidden underneath the hurt. The best thing you can do for yourself is move forward and embrace the freedom. Life doesn't hand you a reset button often, so when it does, make the most of it.

When things aren't going your way, you have two options: throw in the towel, or lift your head up and try again. If at first you don't succeed, dust yourself off and try again. If you let defeat keep you from reaching your goals, you're only doing a disservice to yourself. We weren't put on this earth to be second best, so don't stop trying for the number one spot.

Letting go of your dreams will leave you feeling that you can't accomplish your own goals. By figuring out how to overcome obstacles, you'll prove to the naysayers and to yourself that you can achieve the destiny that's meant for you while you're here on Earth. Let me give you some tips for making a comeback in the midst of trials and tribulations.

- **Grow through what you go through.** Struggle is inevitable. The important thing to realize is that it's not about what you're going through, but about how you're growing through it. I take inspiration from stories of people who have faced difficulties but still managed to end up on top. How you prevail is not about what happens to you: it's how you react to it. Ask yourself if you're learning from your setbacks and becoming a better person because of them.

- **Study your craft.** Find the areas that you feel need work and take the steps you need to improve. It's always possible, and the result will be a reflection of your time and effort: you get out what you put in. Give it your all every time and you'll never fail.

- **Push yourself.** No one is going to do it for you. Some of are lucky enough to have people in our corners providing the encouragement we need to reach the top. While this means a lot, no one in the world can hold your hand and take all the steps to success for you. Encourage yourself, and approach every situation as if it's sink or swim. Other people may not understand your vision, and that's fine: they don't need to. Keep your ultimate goal in mind and be your own motivator.

- **Access your spirituality.** Spirituality can sustain us in times of uncertainty and difficulty. When you don't have the physical, mental, or emotional strength to pull through, your faith in something greater, whatever it may be, can give you the energy you need to keep going. Spirituality reminds us that we are a gift, and we have gifts to offer the world in turn. Our job is to discover these gifts and remove the obstacles to passing them along to others. Focusing on our spirituality helps us to see beyond a setback and find a purpose for it.

- **Give yourself time.** Just as we need to allow time for wounds and broken hearts to mend, we need to give ourselves time to recover from our setbacks. Impatience only makes this process harder and longer than it needs to be. We're always in a hurry to fix our problems and move on, and this impatience can easily become a pattern that spreads into other parts of our lives.

I myself am terribly guilty of impatience, and the only solution I've found is to enjoy other things while I let the setback be resolved in its own time. I try to remember what really matters. I think back to happy memories and keep faith that after the problem is resolved, I'll be where I want to be. It serves no purpose to dwell on a problem. Let the movement of time push you through it. Time does heal!

Remember: when the caterpillar thought its life was over, it started to fly. Do you think it's over? No, my friend, it's just getting started. Sometimes you meet your ultimate pitfall just before you end up on top. I've had moments when I wanted to drop off the face of the Earth. But we're all human. I'm not saying that the punch-in-the-gut feeling won't come again, but it's important to realize that life doesn't have to end there.

STEP 8

KEEP ON SHIFTING

Things are constantly shifting. Loved ones die, jobs end, and so do relationships. People get promoted, couples bond in marriage, and babies are born. Guess what? The good changes can be as hard to adapt to as the bad ones.

How many of us truly accept change? Do we ever really adjust to life willingly? When major changes have come in my life, it's taken me time to make the shift and adjust. Of course, I've always eventually managed to go with the flow and roll with the changes. But now I welcome and accept changes gladly. I've learned to adjust to life on life's terms without unrealistic expectations, and it's made me a much happier and much more content person. I especially love something Gandhi said, and this is the advice I follow now:

> As human beings, our greatness lies not so much in being able to remake the world—that is the myth of the atomic age—as in being able to remake ourselves.

Change is everywhere, and it happens whether we want it or not. Some people welcome change and find ways to turn the unexpected into a chance for growth and development. Others are frightened and react negatively. While we are learning to make a shift, we are still confronted with new and unforeseen changes. Our first reaction may be to run away or fight back—these are survival instincts that take hold when we feel threatened. But once you can adapt mentally, you can formulate a plan and implement it by adjusting to the new situation.

A person who can accept change and adjust to life is one who can focus her mind on new directions and make choices based on the outcomes she wants. But adapting to change is difficult for most people. Humans are creatures of habit, and having to change our habits can be annoying and frustrating. It takes us out of our comfort zone. So when a good change appears, accept it with grace. You may not believe you deserve it, and you might not be ready for it, but the only way to move forward and get the most out of it is to embrace positivity however it shows up.

When a negative change is looming, start looking at your alternatives before it arrives. Be proactive. If you know your company is in trouble and you're hearing things that make you feel insecure about your job, you can start looking for a new one. You might find something better. But even if your position doesn't change, you'll gain valuable experience.

Change is constant, so we usually don't notice the little changes or the expected ones. It's when you're caught off guard that you can get discombobulated. The trick is to remember that this is just one of the millions of changes that will happen to you, and good or not, you have to do what you can to roll with it.

Emotional shifts can be the hardest to adjust to. When your heart is broken, acceptance isn't an easy option, but it's a must if you're to propel through it. Unfortunate encounters like this give you major growing pains but strengthen you emotionally. At the time, though, you may not have the strength or understanding to be objective. You need to process your feelings, and that takes time.

If the changes in your life are overwhelming, you don't have to deal with them all by yourself. Friends, family, support groups, and counselors are available, but you do have to reach out and ask for help, which can also be hard. It may be a struggle, but you don't have to suffer alone. The love of those who care for you can make emotional setbacks much easier. If you hate change, you at least have to tolerate it when it happens. There's no law saying that you have to like it, but you have to find a way to cope, because change happens whether you like it or not.

Imagine sitting in a movie theatre when the lights suddenly go out. You're blind for a few seconds, but gradually you start seeing the objects around you. Your eyes have accepted the change and begun adjusting to the darkness. In the same way, you need to adapt and find new solutions to the problems and situations you encounter.

Life can be hard to navigate in our fast-moving society. Things change so quickly today that by the time you've opened your new laptop and learned all its features, it's obsolete. This guide allows you to deal confidently with the shifts happening around you. It's a great survival tool. We often say, "Surf the waves," and that may be the most comfortable way to deal with the future.

Remember, it's easier to manage change and uncertainty when you keep shifting and adjusting to life and learning new methods, tactics, and strategies.

STEP 9

PROGRESS, NOT PERFECTION

Most of us are trying to reach some sort of goal, even if we haven't fully formulated it in our minds. We want to try something new, break an old habit, or succeed at work. Sometimes these goals are vague in scope and lack a well-defined path to success—mabye a general desire to be healthier, lower our blood pressure, manage our stress, succeed at sports, or be a better friend, spouse, parent, employer, employee, athlete, student, or person. Sometimes, the picture is so big that you don't know what steps will take you there. You may feel you don't have the time or resources.

The simplest notions can be the most powerful. You want to succeed and be recognized for your efforts. But modern society moves quickly, and technology bombards you with the opinions of others. What you need to understand is that some problems simply cannot be remedied overnight. That should make sense—after all, they probably weren't created overnight. Most big problems are the products of years of bad choices. Health problems don't usually appear out of the blue, for instance. They're usually the result of long-term bad habits such as a poor diet or drug or alcohol abuse. Likewise, relationships don't reach a crisis point because of one small conflict. That crisis arises from months or years of self-centered behavior by one or both parties. So, if we can't expect to resolve big problems overnight, we have to look for progress as we move forward rather than perfection.

My health is one area in which I focus on progress rather

than perfection. I exercise regularly—that's one goal I have achieved. But this year, I didn't build my lower body muscles as much as I would have liked. On the other hand, I did kick my caffeine habit. I've also stepped up my cardio, which has improved my stamina, agility, strength, and confidence. I haven't achieved perfection, but I keep making progress toward my goal of being as healthy as I can be. When I began to understand that succeeding was about making today just 1% better than yesterday, things started to flow. You have to start somewhere and be patient with yourself.

You'd be shocked at the results you can achieve from small, daily progress toward a goal. It's easy to forget that sometimes, the best way to learn is by trial and error. No one gets it completely right the first time. Throughout our lives we're either moving closer to our goals or further away from them. That doesn't mean that every misstep and bump in the road turns us around—as long as our general momentum remains forward, we're making progress. It's just when we confuse progress with perfection that we set ourselves up for disappointment.

In that journey of striving, the key thing is to let go of getting it perfectly right. Instead, when you can honestly say that you've tried your best, then you can finish your day feeling fulfilled and wake up refreshed the next morning. Instead of making a slip-up and saying, "I'll start fresh on Monday," get into the mindset that you can still make today better than yesterday, even by a small amount. It's the little efforts and improvements, the ones that seem insignificant at the time, that make all the difference. So, let go of your idea of being perfect and commit to doing your honest best and edging your life closer to where you want it. Celebrate every success and even every failure along the way. As long as you get up, keep trying, and keep making progress, you are winning.

Let me conclude with some thoughts on perfection and progress.

The perfect time to start something never arrives. Procrastination is a symptom of perfection. Perfectionists prefer to wait for the perfect time to do things perfectly rather than doing things when they need to be done. The fear of not doing things perfectly is what pushes them to procrastinate.

Perfection is a moving target. When you strive for excellence, you perform better than you did before. But when you strive for perfection, no matter how much you achieve you are never satisfied.

Strive for progress, not perfection. When you focus on perfection, you worrying at every step. Your focus shifts to possible criticisms and failures. Then you become the roadblock to your own progress. When you strive for progress you succeed faster.

Making mistakes is better than faking perfection: Making mistakes doesn't mean you are a failure. It only means you are trying and learning. So when you make mistakes, learn to accept them and move on.

And finally, as Salvador Dali said, "Have no fear of perfection—you'll never reach it."

CONTACTS

To reach Kathryn McKnight for speaking engagements, coaching, or training, or just to follow her on social media:

P.O. Box 2259

Tampa, FL 33509

Websites

www.accountableactions.com

www.enhancedaccountability.com

www.meetkathymcknight.com

www.dreambodyfit.com

Social Media

Instagram https://bit.ly/2Pa3rBP

YouTube https://bit.ly/2KGdvlz

Facebook https://bit.ly/2rf3GBT

Linked-In https://bit.ly/2Gbvce8

Email

ck@accountableactions.com

www.ingramcontent.com/pod-product-compliance
Lightning Source LLC
Chambersburg PA
CBHW031226090426
42740CB00007B/732